The Learning Works

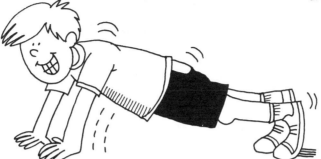

Movin' and Groovin'

Fun exercises to do any time and any place—plus nutrition tips, yummy recipes, and more!

Written by Peggy Buchanan and Linda Schwartz
Illustrated by Kelly Kennedy

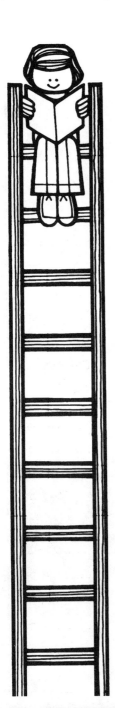

The Learning Works

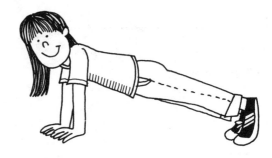

Cover Design & Illustration:
  Kelly Kennedy

Text Design:
  Kimberley A. Clark

Acknowledgments and Dedication

Thank you to Nico Cervantes; Ashley and Adam Lambert; Eleanor McCowen; and Sophie, Sam, and Tom Tischner for testing the activities in this book. Special thanks to Judi Sheppard Missett for bringing out the "kid" in all of us with Jazzercize®.

This book is dedicated to Darrin and Michelle Jensen, to Shelby and Mandy McCowen, and to kids around the world. Have fun with the exercises in this book and may they motivate you to take the first step on the road to a stronger, healthier, and happier YOU!

Copyright © 1997
The Learning Works, Inc.
Santa Barbara, California 93160

ISBN: 0-88160-279-5
LW 349

Printed in the United States of America.

Contents

Contents
(continued)

Contents
(continued)

Calling All Kids!

Movin' and Groovin' is a book filled with unique, creative ways to stay in shape and to get your body moving. The exercises presented are fun and easy to do. No fancy gym or equipment are needed. These exercises and stretches can be done in your bedroom, the kitchen, the family room, or when you're out and about. For example, there's "Beans for Biceps" to do in the kitchen and "Commercial Curls" to do during commercial breaks while you watch television. There are even exercises and stretches you can do in the car while traveling. By doing these exercises as part of your daily routine, you will be on your way to building and improving your muscle strength and endurance. You'll find you have more energy and your body will begin to look better and feel stronger as you get more physically fit.

A fun way to use *Movin' and Groovin'* is to team up with an exercise partner. Your partner can be a best friend, a classmate, your mom or dad, a brother or sister, or a grandparent. You don't have to do these exercises in order. Simply select one you'd like to try and ask your partner to read the directions to you as you do each step. There are illustrations to help you if you want to be sure you're doing a particular movement correctly. Once you've done the exercise a few times, you'll know it by heart and can do it on your own. (Be sure to switch off and have your partner select an exercise to try as you read the directions to him or her.)

You'll also find great recipes for after-school snacks, breakfast, lunch, or dinner. You can prepare these recipes yourself or make them with friends or family members.

Exercises, stretches, nutritional tips, facts about your body, muscle trivia, recipes—they're all here, plus lots more in this fun-filled book. So start movin' and groovin' your way to a stronger and healthier YOU!

A Note to Parents

There is reasonable cause for concern over the declining fitness level of today's kids. This is due in part to decreased physical activity. The average child watches between 15 and 25 hours of television weekly. Recent studies show that more than 40 percent of children have at least one risk factor for heart disease.

The best thing you as a parent can do for your child is to set a good example when it comes to fitness. Children of active parents tend to be more active themselves. Exercise regularly and your kids will follow suit. Finally, although you and your children can't change your inherited physiology, you can remold your psychology. Accept your body type and make it the best it can be!

This book is designed to help teach kids how to balance exercise and eating and the role that activity and food play in healthy, high-energy living. The exercises are fun and easy to do. Have family members work together. While one person reads the steps for performing "Kitchen Curls," other family members can do the exercise. Take turns so that everyone gets to alternate between rest and motion. Make it a point to do a few exercises each day in different parts of the house and when you're out and about. Have your whole family work toward a common goal of fitness and fun!

Note: Check with your family physician before beginning this or any exercise program.

Especially for Teachers

Most of the exercises in this book can be easily adapted and modified for classroom use. These activities are ideal for you to use:

- as a break when switching from one subject to another
- to invigorate your students when they seem sluggish
- to utilize the few minutes before the bell rings for recess, lunch, or dismissal
- as a regular exercise program for your students

Supplies Needed

Ask each student to bring a small pillow from home and an old beach towel to use as a mat. For storage, place these items in a grocery bag with the student's name printed on the outside.

Where to Exercise

- in your classroom if space permits
- in the school multipurpose room
- in the cafeteria (when not in use)
- on the grass if weather permits

Variations

Use your imagination and creativity to adapt these exercises from use in the home to use in your classroom.

Questions About Exercise

- **What is exercise?**

  Exercise is body movement that creates work for the muscles.

- **Why is exercise important?**

  Exercise helps to improve your circulation, helps burn up body fat, and helps you digest your food better. It makes your muscles and bones stronger and it helps relieve tension.

- **What are *isometric* exercises?**

  These are exercises where you tighten and relax your muscles without moving your bones. An example of an isometric exercise is one where you push against a wall or door, tighten your muscles, and then relax your muscles. Isometric exercises are ideal to do when you have to sit or stand for a long period of time and don't have a lot of room for movement.

- **What are *anaerobic* exercises?**

  Anaerobic means "without oxygen." These are exercises where you start and then stop. Gymnastics and calisthenics are examples of anaerobic exercises. Many sports and games you play at school are anaerobic because you have short periods of exertion followed by a period of rest.

Questions About Exercise

(continued)

- **What are *aerobic* exercises?**

    Aerobic means "with oxygen." Aerobic exercises involve movement that continues over a period of time and requires the use of oxygen. Jogging and dancing are examples of aerobic exercise.

- **Should you feel pain when you exercise?**

    Some muscle soreness is normal, especially when you first begin an exercise program and force your muscles beyond their normal range of motion. If pain occurs while you are doing an exercise, however, you should slow down or stop and take a rest.

- **Why do you sweat when you exercise?**

    As your muscles begin to move faster, they produce heat. One way your body cools itself is by releasing some of its water to the skin's surface in the form of sweat. As the moisture collects on your skin, the air passes over it creating a cooling sensation. If you did not sweat when you exercised, your body would become overheated.

Questions About Exercise

(continued)

- **Why does your heart beat faster when you exercise?**

  Muscles require oxygen to work. Your heart is the pumping mechanism that pushes blood through the body to bring oxygen to your muscles. Stronger, faster movements during exercise require more oxygen to be delivered to the muscles. This in turn makes the heart rate speed up. The stronger your heart muscle, the longer you are able to exercise without running out of breath.

- **Are there times when you shouldn't exercise?**

  If you are injured or coming down with a cold or the flu, it is best not to exercise. Give your body a chance to rest. When you feel well enough to begin exercising again, begin slowly and give your body a chance to build itself up again.

- **What are the best ways to avoid injuries when exercising?**

  Do warm-ups before you begin any exercise session. Stretch your muscles and loosen your joints by gently swinging your arms and legs and rolling your head from shoulder to shoulder. Start your exercise program slowly and gradually build up the number of repetitions you do. End each exercise session with a few cool-down stretches.

Fitness Hints for Kids

- Walk to school whenever possible instead of riding in a car.

- Climb stairs whenever you can instead of using an escalator or elevator.

- If you have a dog, play catch and run around with your pet. It's good exercise for both of you.

- Bike, jog, or walk to visit your friends whenever possible instead of riding in a car.

- Exercise with a family member or friend, or plan a hike or bike ride with a group of your friends.

- Vary the activities and exercises you do so you don't get bored. Try new sports, games, or activities.

- Take a 10-minute activity break if you've been sitting for a long time.

- Drink plenty of water before, during, and after exercising—especially on hot days.

- Participate in intramural sports. Join a team and meet new friends while you stay in shape.

- Stretch while you stand in lines—at the movies, at the grocery store, or while waiting for the school bus.

- Set realistic goals for yourself as you start an exercise program.

- Participate in activities you really like—you'll stay with them longer.

- Make an effort to share your fitness experience with a younger child.

Your Comfort Zone

Exercise should be fun and comfortable to do. Here's a list of things you may experience if you push yourself too hard:

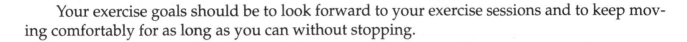

- dizziness
- sore muscles
- injury
- lack of desire to exercise again

Your exercise goals should be to look forward to your exercise sessions and to keep moving comfortably for as long as you can without stopping.

In order to reach your exercise comfort zone, you should be able to answer "yes" to the following questions:

- Is your heart pumping faster?
- Are you breathing faster but not gasping?
- Are you sweating?
- Is your body free of pain?
- Are you improving your skill?
- Are you having fun and looking forward to your next exercise session?

Muscle Chart
(Upper Body)

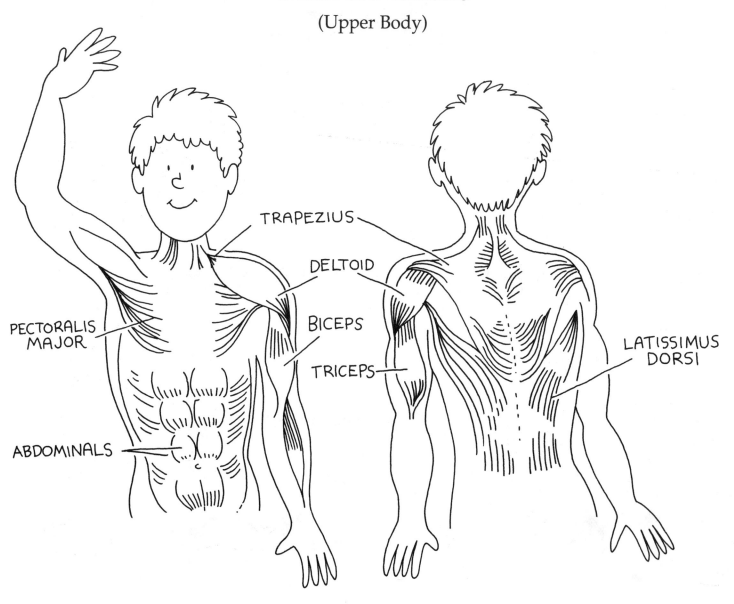

TRAPEZIUS

DELTOID

BICEPS

TRICEPS

PECTORALIS MAJOR

ABDOMINALS

LATISSIMUS DORSI

Muscle Chart

(Lower Body)

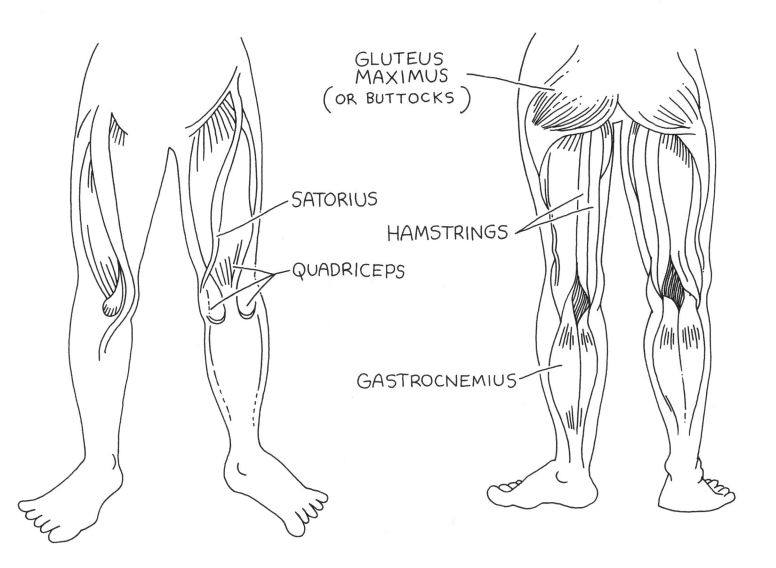

GLUTEUS
MAXIMUS
(OR BUTTOCKS)

SATORIUS

HAMSTRINGS

QUADRICEPS

GASTROCNEMIUS

Meet Your Muscles

Muscles are fibers that contract and relax to make other parts of your body move. Here are some of the muscles in your body.

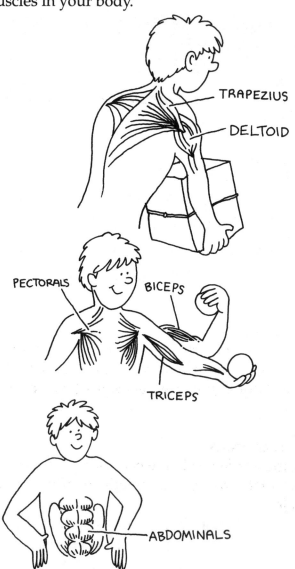

trapezius
holds your shoulder blades, or *scapula*, in place; allows you to shrug your shoulders and pull your shoulder blades together

deltoids
three shoulder muscles that allow you to raise your arms

pectorals
the broad muscles that cover your chest and allow you to cross your arms in front and pull your shoulder blades apart

biceps
the muscles on the front of your upper arm which allow you to bend your arm at the elbow

triceps
the muscles found on the back of your upper arm which allow you to straighten (extend your arm)

abdominals
a group of muscles that cross in different directions from your chest to below your waist and allow you to bend your body at the waist

16

Meet Your Muscles

(continued)

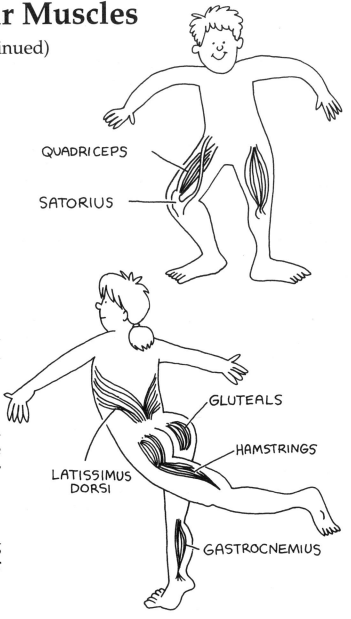

sartorius
the muscle that bends (flexes) your hip and knee joint

quadriceps
muscles found on the upper, front part of your leg (thigh) that allow you to straighten (extend) your knees

latissimus dorsi
muscles running down the sides of your back

gluteals
large muscles in your buttocks that enable you to straighten (extend) your hip joint and stand upright

hamstrings
a group of muscles located behind the thigh that allow you to bend your knee and help the gluteals pull your leg backward (extend your hip)

gastrocnemius
the muscle found in the back of your lower leg (calf) that allows you to straighten (extend) your ankle

QUADRICEPS

SATORIUS

GLUTEALS

HAMSTRINGS

LATISSIMUS DORSI

GASTROCNEMIUS

Muscle Trivia

The *cardiac muscle* makes up most of your heart.

It takes 17 muscles to smile and 43 muscles to make a frown.

The combined weight of all the muscles in your body is about three times as much as that of all your bones.

The largest mass of muscles in your body is your gluteals (buttocks muscles).

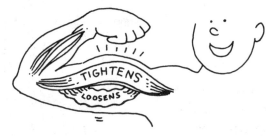

Skeletal muscles work in pairs. When one muscle *contracts* or tightens, the other muscle relaxes.

The muscle that closes your jaw is called the *masseter* muscle. It is one of the strongest muscles in your body.

Muscle Fitness

Here are some important terms to help you
understand how to measure the fitness of your muscles.

Muscle Endurance

Muscle endurance is how well a particular group of muscles
can work for a long period of time. Muscle endurance can be
measured in several ways. One way is to see how many times
you can repeat an exercise in a number of seconds or minutes
(such as the number of sit-ups you can do in three minutes).
Another way to measure muscle endurance is to see how long
you can maintain a certain position over a period of time.

Muscle Strength

Muscle strength is the maximum amount of work your muscles
can do in a single effort, such as lifting a weight, hitting a base-
ball, or doing a standing broad jump.

Flexibility

Flexibility is the amount of movement your muscles can make in
any direction around a joint. One test of flexibility involves bending over to see how close you can come to touching your toes.

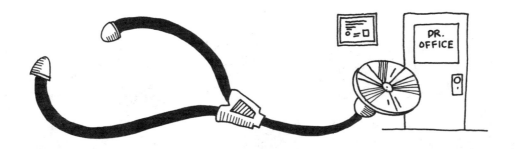

Before You Begin

Check with your family physician before beginning this or any other exercise program, especially if you have health conditions that should be taken into consideration. If you don't understand how to do a particular exercise, ask someone older to go through the steps with you.

Whenever you are exercising, be careful not to overheat your body. If your body gets so hot you feel dizzy, light-headed, or nauseous, you may be experiencing heat stroke. Immediately sit down, cool off, and drink lots of fluids.

Exercises in the Bedroom

A Note on Stretching

Stretching feels good when it is done correctly. Stretching is not stressful. It should be peaceful, relaxing, and noncompetitive. Each person's range of motion (flexibility) depends on how his or her body is put together. Some people can bend farther in certain directions than other people. Just because you may not be able to bend forward and touch your toes with your legs straight, doesn't mean you aren't good at stretching. It may mean your ligaments are shorter and/or your joints won't allow you to bend that far. Do the stretches in this chapter to the best of your ability. You will become more flexible as you practice. Remember to stretch slowly as far as you can without causing pain, and hold the stretch while you count to 30. Don't hold your breath. Relax and breath easily when you stretch.

Pillow Presses

This exercise helps to relax your body
from the top of your thighs up to your chest.

What You Do

1. Lie face down on your bed with a pillow under your stomach.

2. Place your hands palms down at shoulder level with your elbows bent, as shown.

3. Slowly press with your arms, lifting your head and chest off the bed as far as you can, keeping your hips on the bed.

4. If you are doing this stretch correctly, you should not feel any strain in your lower back.

HIPS STAY
ON BED

5. Hold the position for a count of 10.

6. Slowly lower your body back onto the bed.

7. Repeat. Slowly try to build up to 5-10 repetitions at one time.

Star Stretcher

This stretch will help to relax your entire body. It's a great one to do when you come home from a hard day at school, after a rigorous soccer practice, or just to help you unwind at the end of the day.

What You Do

1. Lie on your bed face up.

2. Straighten your arms and legs. Point each limb to a corner of your bed, as shown.

3. Reach as far as you can in all four directions at the same time. Hold this position as you slowly count to 10. Breathe normally as you hold this position.

4. Can you stretch and reach just a little bit more toward the four corners of the bed? Give it a try.

5. As you stretch, think about something that makes you smile. (Smiling is a good stretch for your face!)

6. Now let your arms and legs go limp. Relax all the muscles in your body.

7. Repeat the Star Stretcher. Continue until your star begins to fade.

Tootsie Twists

Here's a great exercise for sore, tired feet.

What You Do

1. Lie on your back on your bed or on the floor.

2. Straighten your legs and point your toes away from your body.

3. Without lifting your legs off the bed, flex (bend) your ankles so your toes are pointing up toward the ceiling.

4. Rotate both feet so that your toes make large circles.

5. Spread your toes as far apart as you can and make 6 clockwise circles with your feet.

6. Now squeeze your toes together as tightly as you can and make 6 counterclockwise circles.

7. Repeat steps 3–6 until your toes, feet, or ankles begin to tire. Build up to 30 repetitions in one sitting.

Scarecrow Swivel

This is a great stretch for your lower back and hips. The slow, rotating action helps prepare your spine for actions that involve twisting, such as batting, throwing a ball, and dancing.

What You Do

1. Lie on your bed with your knees bent and your feet flat on the bed close to your buttocks.

2. Put your arms straight out at your sides from your shoulders so you look like a scarecrow.

3. Keeping your knees together, gently drop both legs to one side.

4. Keep your shoulders flat on the bed and your chest open to the ceiling. Hold for a count of 10. Only stretch as far as is comfortable for your back.

5. Bring your bent knees back to the center of your chest before repeating the Scarecrow Swivel on the other side. Do 10 repetitions on each side.

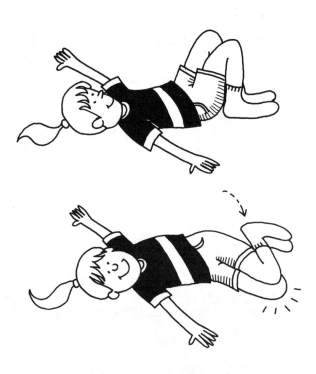

Snug as a Bug

This exercise helps to stretch the muscles
in your lower back. It's an easy exercise to do in bed
or on the floor while you're watching television.

What You Do

1. Lie on your back and pull your right knee
toward your chest with your hands grasped
underneath your knee.

2. Keep your head and upper back flat on the
bed while you bring your knee across your
chest toward your left shoulder. Hold this
position for a count of 10.

3. Switch sides and repeat by bringing your
left knee across your chest to your right
shoulder.

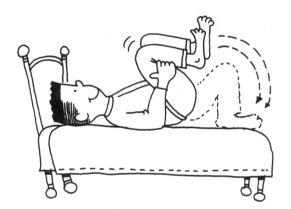

4. After you have stretched each side, repeat
the stretch using both legs. Lie on your back
with both knees bent and your feet flat on
the bed next to your buttocks.

5. Place both hands under your knees and pull them slowly and firmly against your chest.

6. Lower your legs and begin again. Be careful not to straighten your knees while lowering
your legs.

Ceiling Stretches

Here's a great stretch for the back of your legs.
This exercise feels good when your muscles are tired or sore
from running, jumping, rollerblading, in-line skating, or just playing hard.

What You Do

1. Lie on your bed flat on your back.

2. Place both hands under your knees and pull them slowly and firmly against your chest.

3. Keeping your knees bent, grab your toes with both hands, as shown.

4. Still holding onto your toes, slowly begin to straighten your legs. Don't let go! Keep your feet flexed (bent at the ankles) with your heels pointed to the ceiling. Only straighten your legs as far as you comfortably can. Hold this position for a count of 10. If your legs begin to shake, hold that position and don't go any further.

5. Bend your knees and begin again. Do 10 Ceiling Stretches.

Pillow Pulls

This exercise strengthens your abdominals while it stretches your back.
It's a balancing act for overall good posture which will help you perform better in all sports.

What You Do

1. Lie face down on your bed with your pillow under your head.

2. Keeping your legs together and straight, place your hands next to your head on your pillow, as shown.

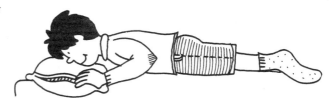

3. Slowly press with your arms, lifting your body off of the bed. (Keep your hands and knees in contact with the bed.)

4. Sit back on your heels as you pull your pillow toward your knees while lowering your buttocks to your feet, as shown.

5. Return to your starting position. Repeat pillow pulls 10 times.

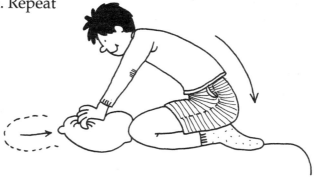

Sleepy Stork

This exercise helps stretch the muscles on the front of your thighs and the muscles that flex your hips. Activities like walking, kicking, and running can make these muscles very tight. If these muscles are not stretched often, your back can feel tired and sore.

What You Do

1. Lie face down on your bed with your legs straight. Turn your head to the side so you can breathe easily.

2. Slowly bend your right knee, lifting your right heel toward your buttocks.

3. Lightly grasp your right foot with your right hand, keeping both hips flat on the bed.

4. Gently pull your foot toward your buttocks, keeping the foot in line with the knee and the knee in line with the hip, as shown.

5. Hold for a count of 10. Return to your starting position and repeat the stretch with your other leg.

6. After you have stretched each leg, try stretching both legs at the same time.

Laundry Shoot

This exercise improves your balance. Good balance is necessary in many activities, such as gymnastics, dancing, surfing, skateboarding, and rollerblading. To do this exercise, you'll need a hamper or laundry basket and some dirty laundry that needs to be picked up off the floor.

What You Do

1. Find some laundry that's been left around your bedroom. Stand on one foot near the laundry. Straighten your arms out to the sides to help you keep your balance. Extend your other leg straight behind you and lift it as high as you can without losing your balance.

2. When you feel you have your balance, lean forward and pick up the first laundry item.

3. Toss it into your laundry basket.

4. Alternate legs until all of your dirty laundry has landed in the basket.

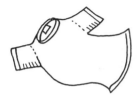 

Mattress Dips

This is a great exercise for your chest, the back of your arms, and the front of your shoulders.

What You Do

1. Stand at the side of your bed, facing away from the mattress. Stand with your feet slightly apart about three feet away from the bed so your body is at a slant. (Don't stand on an area rug, which might slip.)

2. Place your hands on the mattress with your fingers pointing forward and your elbows straight.

3. Bend your elbows and your knees; at the same time, lower your buttocks toward the floor until your elbows and knees have reached a 90° angle.

4. Lift your body up with your arms until your arms straighten all the way and you have returned to a standing position.

5. Repeat 8 to 12 times or until you are tired.

Mattress Push-Ups

This exercise is great for improving your coordination and strengthening your chest muscles.

What You Do

1. Stand at the side of your bed, facing your mattress. Stand with your feet slightly apart about three feet away from the bed so your body is at a slant, as shown. (Don't stand on an area rug, which might slip.)

2. Place your hands on the mattress with your elbows bent, shoulder-width apart, as shown. Your chest will be resting on the side of the bed.

3. Push your chest off the mattress without bending at the hips as you straighten your arms. Then lower your chest back to its original position.

4. Repeat 8 to 12 times or until you are tired.

5. For an added challenge, try pushing yourself off the bed high enough to clap your hands once or twice before returning to your original position.

Spiral Spins

The first part of this exercise stretches the back of the thighs, or hamstrings. The latter part stretches the front of your thighs, or quadriceps, and helps you improve your balance.

What You Do

1. Stand facing the side of your bed with your shoes off.

2. Raise one leg and place your foot on your mattress, as shown.

3. Gently lean forward at the hips while straightening the leg that is on the bed.

4. Hold the stretch for a count of 10. (Don't press down on your knee with your hands.) Return to your starting position.

5. Repeat the stretch with your other leg.

6. Each time you do this stretch, add another count of 10 until you can hold this position for one minute.

Spiral Spins

(continued)

7. Slowly make a half-turn facing away from your bed, as shown. The top of your foot and toes should press against your mattress.

8. Stand erect with your back leg as straight as possible until you feel a slight stretch in your hip and thigh.

9. Hold this position for a count of 10. Return to your starting position.

10. Repeat the stretch with your other leg.

Balancing Act

This is a great drill to improve your overall balance and flexibility. Good balance and flexibility are necessary for most sports, especially surfing, skateboarding, rollerblading, ballet, and gymnastics.

What You Do

1. Try standing on one leg and putting your sock and shoe on the other foot.

2. The first few times you try this, you may have to hold onto something stationary with one hand.

3. Practice until you can put both shoes on without holding onto anything.

4. For an added challenge, close your eyes as you do this activity.

Elbow Push-Ups

Doing this exercise is great way to strengthen your abdominal muscles. When you have strong "abs," you have a healthier back and better posture.

What You Do

1. Lie face down on the floor with your legs straight and together. Place your elbows directly under your shoulders, with your forearms on the floor and your hands clasped together, as shown.

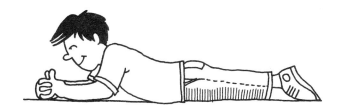

2. Raise your body from the floor by lifting your hips, creating a straight line from your head to your heels. (In the "up" position, your body should be in a straight line and your elbows, forearms, and toes should be in contact with the floor.)

3. Lower your body to the starting position. Keep your head up throughout the exercise.

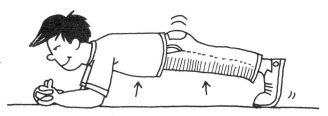

4. Repeat 8-12 times or until you get tired.

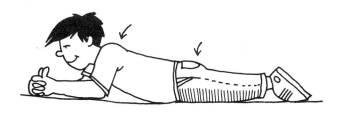

Over the Edge

This exercise strengthens the muscles in your buttocks, which are called the gluteals.

What You Do

1. Lie face down on your bed with your hips barely on the edge and your legs over the side of the bed, as shown.

2. Place your arms straight down next to your sides with your palms face down on the bed.

3. Slowly lift one leg as high as you can straight out behind you.

4. Repeat 8-12 times before switching sides.

5. For an additional challenge, try slowly lifting both legs at the same time. Be sure to tighten your abdominal muscles and keep your head on the bed while you lift your legs.

6. For an even greater challenge, put bean bag weights on your ankles. (See the directions for making bean bag weights on pages 134–135.)

38

Catnap Stretch

Have you ever seen a cat round and arch its back in a long, lazy stretch?
Here's your chance to mimic a cat and stretch your back and abdominals—a great
waker-upper on those mornings you don't want to get out of bed.

What You Do

1. Position yourself on your bed on your hands and knees with your knees directly under your hips and your hands, palms down, under your shoulders.

2. Round your back as high as you can, like a cat stretching after a nap. Press up as high as you can but don't lift your hands off the bed.

3. Let your head fall forward naturally. Hold for a count of 10.

4. Now pull your chest down toward your bed, arching your back.

5. Bend your elbows slightly while you lift your chin and point your buttocks toward the ceiling. Hold for a count of 10. Repeat the Catnap Stretch 10 times alternating up and down in a smooth motion.

39

Towel Stretches

You don't need any fancy exercise equipment for these stretches.
Just grab a hand towel and you're ready to go!

What You Do

1. Stand or sit tall while holding the end of a hand towel in your right hand. Bend your elbow behind your head so the towel hangs down toward the floor, as shown.

2. Bend your left arm behind your back, grasping the loose end of the towel with your other hand.

3. Gently straighten your left arm toward the floor until you feel a comfortable stretch on the back of your right arm.

4. Hold this position for 10 seconds, tightening your abdominal muscles to avoid arching your back.

5. Now straighten your right arm above your head and bend your left arm behind your back until you feel a gentle stretch on the front of your left shoulder. Hold this position for 10 seconds.

6. Switch sides and repeat.

Towel Stretches

(continued)

Variation 1—Towel Turnaround

1. In a standing position, hold the hand towel with both hands in front of your hips, palms facing back.

2. With hands a bit wider than shoulder width, grasp the towel and slowly raise your arms overhead and down behind your back, as shown.

3. Slowly lift your arms back up and over to the starting position.

4. Your hands should be far enough apart to allow free movement up and over your head.

5. Repeat several times.

6. For an even greater stretch, move your hands slightly closer together.

Variation 2—Towel Torso Stretch

1. In a standing position, hold the hand towel lengthwise in front of you about shoulder level.

2. Lift your arms toward the ceiling until they reach a position slightly above your head, as shown.

3. Keeping your abdominals tight and your knees slightly bent, slowly bend sideways without twisting. Your arms should remain straight and slightly above your head. Hold for 10 seconds.

4. Return to the starting position. Repeat the stretch by bending toward the other side. Be careful not to twist your back.

Laundry Lifts

This exercise strengthens your arms and shoulders.

What You Do

1. Stand up straight holding a laundry bag or a pillowcase that contains a few unbreak-able items.

2. Begin with your arms straight down in front of you, palms facing your body.

3. Lift the pillowcase or laundry bag by bending your elbows until your hands reach your chin.

4. Lower the bag until your arms are straight again.

5. Repeat 8-12 times.

Exercises in the Kitchen

Beans for Biceps

Use cans of beans to build your biceps.
Think how much easier it will be to take out the garbage,
lift heavy objects, and haul baskets of laundry with stronger biceps!

What You Do

1. Use two cans of beans (16 ounces) for weights. (If you have smaller hands, use smaller cans.)

2. Stand with your feet shoulder-width apart. Hold a can of beans in each hand.

3. Start this exercise with your arms straight down and your hands by your sides, palms facing forward.

4. Keeping your arms by your sides, bend your elbows and bring the weights up to your shoulders, as shown. Stand straight and tall as you do this exercise.

5. Slowly lower your hands to the starting position.

6. Repeat this exercise 10 times.

Variations to Beans for Biceps

Here are two variations you can do based on Beans for Biceps.

Variation 1

1. Stand with your feet shoulder-width apart. Hold a can of beans in each hand with your palms facing your body.

2. Keeping your elbows close to your sides, lift your arms straight forward and up until they reach shoulder level but are still in front of your face.

3. Slowly lower your arms to the starting position. Repeat 10 times.

Variation 2

1. Stand with your feet shoulder-width apart. Hold a can of beans in each hand with your palms facing your body. Lift your arms straight back and up as high as you can without bending forward. (You won't be able to lift your arms as high as you did in Variation 1.)

2. Stand straight and tall. Keep your chin tucked in.

3. Slowly lower your arms to the starting position. Repeat 10 times.

Tomatoes for Triceps

Your triceps are located on the back of your upper arm. Having strong triceps will help you throw farther, bat harder, and hit a mean backhand in tennis.

What You Do

1. Grab two 16-ounce cans of tomatoes. (Use smaller cans if your hands are smaller.) Hold a can in each hand.

2. Stand with your feet shoulder-width apart. Start with the cans straight up over your head with your palms facing back.

3. Keep your elbows up and facing forward.

4. Slowly bend your elbows (without letting them fall forward) and lower the cans to your shoulders with your palms facing down.

5. Extend your arms straight up overhead to the starting position.

6. Repeat 10 times.

Kitchen Dippers

This exercise is a good overall upper-body strengthener.

What You Do

1. Sit up straight on the front edge of a chair that has arms at the sides.

2. Grip the arms of the chair with both hands. Keep your elbows bent at 90° and your feet flat on the floor.

3. Tighten your abdominal muscles and lift your chest.

4. Keeping your knees bent, lift your body with your arms until your arms straighten all the way and your buttocks comes off the seat.

5. With straight arms supporting you, lower your body until your elbows form right angles and your buttocks returns to the seat.

6. Repeat 10 times.

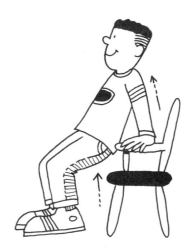

Submarine Sinks

Next time you dash into the kitchen for an afternoon or evening snack,
try this version of a push-up that's easy, fun to do, and a good upper-body builder!

What You Do

1. Stand in front of your kitchen sink or counter. Be sure to remove any area rugs so you don't slip.

2. Place your hands on the sink or countertop, shoulder distance apart as shown. Turn your fingertips in slightly.

3. Stand with your feet together about three feet away from the base of the counter so your body is at a slant.

Submarine Sinks

(continued)

4. Slowly lower your chest to the sink or countertop, bending your arms as you go. Be sure to keep your back straight and your head up. Then slowly push yourself back to your starting position, as shown.

5. Start with 8 repetitions. Build up the number of Submarine Sinks you do each time you find yourself standing by the kitchen sink or counter.

6. For an added challenge, try Submarine Sinks with your feet further away from the counter. (Don't go back too far or you'll find yourself face down on the kitchen floor!)

Wall Rollers

This is a relaxing exercise that will feel good
after washing dishes or putting away groceries.

What You Do

1. Stand with your head, back, and hips against a wall.

2. Place your feet about one foot away from the wall.

3. Gently drop your chin to your chest and very slowly roll your spine down and away from the wall, one inch at a time. Don't allow your hands to drop below knee level.

4. Keep your hips against the wall and your abdominal muscles tight.

5. Let your arms hang forward, as shown, and breathe naturally.

6. Tighten your abdomen even more as you roll your spine back up the wall, one inch at a time, until you reach your original position.

7. Repeat 10 times.

The Kitchen Wall Walker

Here's an exercise that will strengthen the muscles
in your legs for running, jumping, hiking, and skiing.

What You Do

1. Find an empty space on a kitchen wall with
   plenty of room on both sides.

2. Stand straight and tall with your back
   against the wall.

3. Slowly slide your upper body down the
   wall. At the same time, walk your feet out
   away from the wall until you look like you
   are sitting in an imaginary chair.

4. Your hips and knees should be at a 90°
   angle, as shown.

5. Hold this position for a count of 10.

6. Now walk your feet back toward the wall as
   you slide your upper body back to a
   standing position.

7. If your knees begin to hurt, don't slide
   down so far.

8. Repeat 10 times or until you begin to feel
   tired.

Kitchen Crunches

This exercise is great for strengthening your arms, thighs, and abdominal muscles.

What You Do

1. Sit all the way back in a kitchen chair.

2. Grasp the arms of the chair or the bottom of the seat on both sides.

3. Push down with your arms as you lift your buttocks up off the chair seat.

4. Tuck your knees to your chest, as shown, and hold for a count of 10.

5. Return to your starting position and repeat 10 times.

6. As an added challenge, slowly straighten your legs out in front of you, parallel to the floor. Hold for another count of 10.

7. For an even harder workout, try doing this exercise with bean bag weights on your ankles. (See the directions for making bean bag weights on pages 134–135.)

Toe Grabbers

The muscles on the bottom of your feet need exercise just like the muscles in your arms and legs. A barefoot walk on a sandy beach is one of the best exercises you can do. But if it's winter or you don't live by the beach, this exercise is for you!

What You Do

1. Place a paper towel or an old dish towel flat on the floor.

2. Take off your shoes and wiggle your toes.

3. Begin by placing your right foot at one end of the towel. Grab the edge of the towel with your toes and gather it up as you pull it under the arch of your foot.

4. Reverse the motion and flatten the towel to its original position. Repeat 10 times.

5. Repeat the exercise with your left foot.

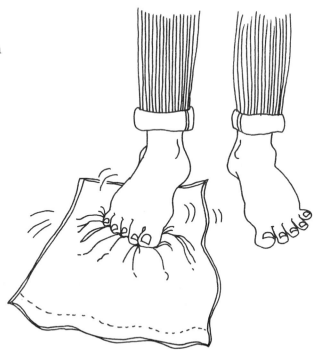

Souper Arm Lifts

This exercise helps to strengthen the top of your shoulders and the upper part of your arms.

What You Do

1. Use two cans of soup from your kitchen pantry. (If you don't have any soup handy, use two equal-size cans of fruits or vegetables.)

2. Stand in the kitchen with your feet shoulder-width apart.

3. Grasp a can in each hand, keeping your arms straight down at your sides with your palms facing your body.

4. Slowly lift your arms up and straight out to the side until they reach shoulder level. Your palms should be facing down as you grasp the cans of soup, as shown.

5. Slowly lower your arms to your starting position.

6. Repeat 10 times.

7. As you increase your strength and this exercise becomes easier, add more repetitions or use heavier cans.

Door Jammer

Doing this exercise will help you to strengthen the muscles on the back of your shoulders and between your shoulder blades. This activity will also help you improve your posture.

What You Do

1. Find an open doorway in your kitchen. Stand in the doorway with your feet shoulder-width apart and your back leaning against the door jam.

2. Position yourself so that the jam is between your shoulder blades. Lift your arms straight up to shoulder level.

3. Reach behind you with both arms and touch the walls on either side of the door jam, as shown, and hold for a count of 10. (Keep your head against the door jam and try not to lean forward.)

4. Repeat the stretch 5-10 times.

Corner Crunch

This exercise stretches your chest muscles and helps you stand tall for super posture!

What You Do

1. Find a kitchen corner you can stand in. Stand facing the corner with your feet shoulder-width apart about three feet from the wall.

2. Place one hand at shoulder level on each wall.

3. Pull your shoulder blades together and press both elbows back as you lean into the corner with all your weight, as shown.

4. Make sure your movements are slow and controlled.

5. Hold this position for 30 seconds. Repeat the stretch 5-10 times.

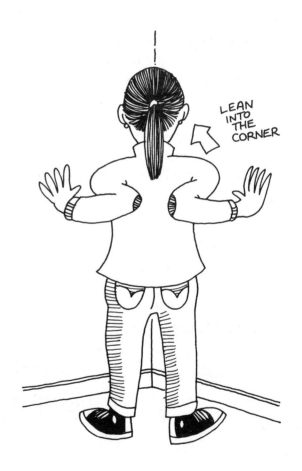

LEAN INTO THE CORNER

Clean Sweep

Games can make chores more fun to do. Try Clean Sweep the next time
you sweep or mop to exercise the muscles in your arms, sides, and back.
Like any other exercise, you should do the same number of repetitions on each side.

What You Do

1. Look at the floor you want to sweep or mop
   and make a guess as to how many sweeps it
   will take to get the job done.

2. Cut the number in half and alternate sides
   as you sweep or mop. Example: If you think
   it will take 100 sweeps to clean the kitchen
   floor, do 50 strokes on the left and 50 on the
   right.

3. If the floor isn't completely clean, keep
   sweeping or mopping until the job is done.

4. You can also do Clean Sweep as you listen
   to your favorite music.

Kitchen Clock Kicks

This exercise will help improve your hip flexibility and overall balance.
This exercise is something you might do in a ballet or karate class.

What You Do

1. Stand sideways next to a counter in your kitchen. Place your hand on the counter for balance.

2. Lift the leg that is away from the counter straight forward until it is parallel to the floor. Point your toe straight ahead as if it were the big hand on a clock striking 12 o'clock, as shown.

3. Hold this position for 10 seconds.

4. Return your leg to the original position and pause for a moment.

58

Kitchen Clock Kicks

(continued)

5. Slowly lift the same leg straight out to the side (toward the nine o'clock position) and point your toe. In this position, your leg will only lift to about 45°.

6. Return your leg to its original position and pause for another moment.

7. Slowly extend your leg behind you, pointing your toe toward the six o'clock position. (Lift your leg as high as you can without bending forward.)

8. Return to your original position.

9. Turn your other side to the counter. Place your hand on the counter for balance and repeat steps 2–8 with your other leg.

10. For an added challenge, hold for longer than 10 seconds and flex your foot before returning to your original position. To get an even greater workout, attach bean bag weights to your ankles. (See the directions for making bean bag weights on pages 134–135.)

Counter Calf and Quad Stretches

Doing these two stretches is a great way to prevent muscle tightness
after a lot of walking, running, or jumping.

What You Do

1. Stand facing your kitchen counter with one foot in front of the other in a lunge position. The foot closest to the counter should be about two feet away from the base of the counter while the other foot is about that same distance behind it, as shown.

2. Place both hands on the counter shoulder-width apart with your fingers pointing forward and your elbows slightly bent.

3. Brace yourself against the counter while you press the heel of your back foot flat against the floor.

4. Your front knee should be bent while all of your weight is on your extended back leg.

5. Hold this stretch for a count of 30.

6. Switch legs and repeat steps 1–5.

PRESS BACK

60

Counter Calf and Quad Stretches

(continued)

7. After you have stretched both of your calves, bend one leg behind you and place your foot in your hand, as shown. Your other hand should remain on the counter for balance.

8. Make sure both of your hips are facing the counter directly in front of you.

9. Point your knee directly toward the floor as you press your body slightly forward without twisting to either side.

10. Hold this stretch for a count of 30. Switch sides and repeat.

 # Ham Hocks

Your hamstrings are the muscles you use when flexing or bending your knees. They are located at the back of your thighs. The large muscle group on the front of the thigh is called the quadriceps. Your quadriceps muscles are usually much stronger than your hamstrings. When there is an imbalance in muscle strength, injuries are more likely to occur. By taking extra time to strengthen the hamstrings, you are less likely to experience a pull or tear when sprinting, kicking, or lunging quickly in sports or play.

What You Do

1. Stand tall facing the sink, counter, or the back of a chair. Hold on for balance.

2. Place your feet shoulder-width apart.

3. Without bending at the hip, lift your right heel up to the right side of your buttocks while bending your right knee.

4. Return to the starting position and repeat 8-12 times. Switch sides and repeat the exercise with your left leg.

5. For an added challenge, strap bean bag weights to your ankles. (See the directions for making bean bag weights on pages 134–135.)

Stand Up, Sit Down

Here's an exercise that will help you strengthen your heart as well as the muscles in your legs and buttocks.

What You Do

1. Sit on the edge of a chair with your feet flat on the floor and your hands resting on your thighs.

2. Put your right hand on your left shoulder for count 1 and hold it there while you put your left hand on your right shoulder for count 2.

3. On the count of 3, uncross your left arm and place your hand back on your left thigh. Now place your right hand on your right thigh for count 4.

4. On the count of 5, stand up and clap your hands over your head, then sit down and slap your thighs for count 6. Repeat standing up and sitting down for counts 7 and 8.

5. Repeat the entire sequence 8-12 times or until your legs feel tired.

6. For an added challenge, extend your legs straight out in front of you and hold them there as you place your hands on your shoulders. Bend your knees and put your feet back on the floor as you place your hands on your thighs.

Freezer Squeezers

Did you know that your freezer or refrigerator can help you get fit?
Try this fun isometric exercise to find out how.

What You Do

1. Stand facing your freezer close enough to grab both sides of it with your hands, as shown.

2. Take a deep breath then press your hands and arms together as if you were playing an accordion or giving your freezer a big hug. Squeeze as hard as you can for a count of 10 as you exhale, then relax.

3. Now stand with your back to the freezer.

4. Reach around behind you and grasp both sides of the freezer without bending forward.

5. Take a deep breath and press your hands and arms together for a count of 10, then exhale.

6. Feel the muscles in your chest, arms and back get very tense before you let go.

Note: Isometric exercises can make you feel very strong. Be careful not to lift or move the freezer or refrigerator!

Exercises in the Family Room

Cut a Card for Fitness

This is a fun activity you and your family can do while watching television or when you're stuck in the house on a rainy day. You will need a deck of playing cards for this activity.

What You Do

1. Decide who will choose the exercise and who will select the card.

2. Thumb through this book and pick any exercise.

3. Cut the deck of cards in half and turn the top card over so the number is face up.

4. Everybody does the chosen exercise the number of times shown on the card. If a face card shows (jack, queen, or king) do the exercise for 10 repetitions. If the activity picked is a stretch, hold the desired position for the number of seconds indicated on the card (or for 10 seconds if a face card shows).

5. For fun, shuffle the two jokers into the deck. If a joker appears, the person who picks the cards decides how many repetitions will be done. (The person who selected the card must also do the exercise!)

6. If you're watching television, try to pick at least one card per commercial.

 # Frog Stand

It may take some practice to be able to get into this position, but just trying to do it will help you improve your overall strength, coordination, and balance.

What You Do

1. Get on your hands and knees on a carpeted floor.

2. Place your head on the floor slightly in front of and between your hands, as shown.

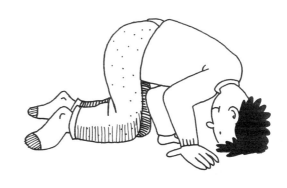

3. Lean forward on your head, placing one knee at a time onto each elbow and lifting your feet off the floor until you have created a tripod with your two hands and your head. (See illustration.)

4. Remain in this position only until you have gained enough balance to lift your head and balance on your hands like a frog on a lily pad.

RIBBIT

Turkey Stretch

This is a great stretch to relax your lower back and your buttocks.
After you do this activity, see if you can guess why it's called Turkey Stretch!

What You Do

1. Lie on your back and tuck your knees into your chest.

2. Cross your right ankle over your left ankle. Grasp your right ankle with your left hand and left ankle with your right hand. (Be sure to grasp your ankles and not your feet.) This will keep you from putting too much stress on your ankle joints.

3. Pull your knees firmly toward your chest.

4. Without uncrossing your ankles, pull your feet apart and hold for a count of 10.

5. Uncross your ankles and put your left ankle over your right ankle. Hold this position for another count of 10.

TUCK KNEES INTO CHEST

CROSS ANKLES

Turkey Stretch

(continued)

Variation—Half Turkey Stretch

1. Lie on your back with your knees bent and your feet flat on the bed close to your buttocks. Keep your arms out to the side, like the wings of an airplane.

2. Place your right ankle on your left knee so that your right knee points out to the side, as shown.

3. Now bring your left knee up to your chest as far as you comfortably can. Hold for a count of 30.

4. Switch sides and begin again.

Lift-Off

Try this exercise to help you improve your balance.

What You Do

1. Get on your hands and knees on a carpeted floor.

2. Lift one leg off the floor straight out behind you and point your toe.

3. Keep your leg lifted and extend your opposite arm straight out in front of you as high as you can while maintaining your balance, as shown.

4. Hold this position for as long as you can. Try to work up to one minute.

5. Repeat on the other side.

6. For an added challenge, try lifting your leg and arm on the same side.

V-Sits

These exercises help you improve your balance and strengthen your abdominal muscles.

What You Do

1. Sit tall on the floor with your legs together and extended forward.

2. Raise your arms over your head, creating an "L" shape with your body.

3. Slowly lean back on your buttocks, lifting both legs and changing the shape of your body from an "L" to a "V."

4. Hold this position for as long as you can.

5. Rest for 60 seconds and repeat steps 1-4 three times.

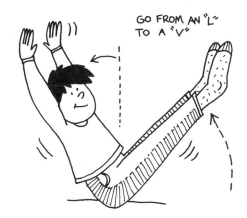

GO FROM AN "L" TO A "V"

Variation—V-Sit Challenge

1. Lie flat on the floor face up with your arms over your head, palms up, as shown.

2. Tuck your legs in close to your chest, then straighten them toward the ceiling, creating an "L" shape with your body.

3. With your feet together, lower your legs halfway to the floor as you roll your spine off the floor, one inch at a time, creating a "V" with your entire body, as shown.

4. Balance on your buttocks for a moment, then slowly roll down to your original position.

5. Repeat three times.

ROLL FORWARD INTO A "V"

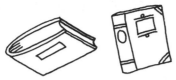

Book Balance

Next time you're reading a book, take a fitness break with this activity.
Mark your place and close your book. With this balancing act,
you'll stay alert and improve your posture.

What You Do

1. Sit tall and place your book on top of your head.

2. When you feel you have the book balanced on your head, slowly stand up.

3. Walk around the room with the book balanced on your head.

4. For an added challenge, try balancing on one foot as you lift your other leg either forwards or backwards. Don't forget to sit down and finish your reading!

Couch Curls

Here's a great exercise to do during commercials when you're watching television. This exercise helps to strengthen your abdominal muscles.

What You Do

1. Lie on the floor with your legs resting on the seat and your buttocks against the front of a couch or chair, as shown.

2. Fold your arms across your chest.

3. Keeping your chin tucked slightly toward your chest, lift your shoulder blades off the floor and try to touch the bottom of your ribs to the top of your hips. (Make sure your legs do not leave the couch.) To prevent yourself from forcing your neck too far forward, do a "neck check." Place your fist between your chin and your chest. Rest your chin lightly on your thumb and your little finger on your chest.

4. Exhale as you lift your shoulders off the floor. Don't hold your breath. Return to your starting position.

5. Continue doing Couch Curls until you have done as many as you can. Then try to do just one more.

Commercial Circles

This exercise puts your shoulder and upper-back muscles to work. Notice that you only circle your arms backwards, which counteracts the typical forward "slouch" position of television viewing.

What You Do

1. Stand tall with feet shoulder width apart. Tighten your abdominal muscles and buttocks so your hips don't tip forward.

2. Hold your arms straight up and out to the side no higher than shoulder level.

3. Lift your shoulders up, back, down, and forward, making a circle with your entire arm.

4. Repeat 8-12 times alternating palms facing down, palms forward, and palms up.

5. If you find this activity too difficult, lower your arms to your side and gradually work up to the higher level.

6. If you can do this exercise with ease, challenge yourself by doing Commercial Circles while holding a can of beans in each hand. (Don't spill the beans! Make sure you have a good grip on the cans before you start making circles.)

MOVE YOUR SHOULDERS & ARMS IN A CIRCLE

74

Bottoms Up

This exercise strengthens the back of your thighs and your buttocks.
Since many daily activities focus on the front of your thighs, it is important
to build the muscles on the back of your thighs so they will be equally strong.

What You Do

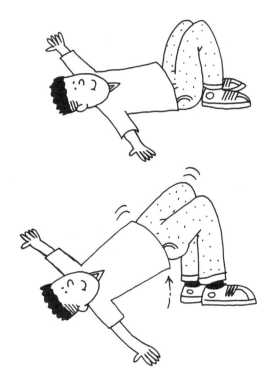

1. Lie on the floor face up with your knees bent and your feet close to your buttocks. Straighten your arms out to the side.

2. Lift your hips off the floor until you make a straight line from your knees to your shoulders, as shown.

3. Tighten the muscles in your buttocks as you lift. Be careful not to arch your back. Put your body's weight on your shoulders not your neck. Hold this position for a few seconds before lowering your body to the starting position.

4. Repeat 8-12 times or until you feel tired.

5. For an added challenge, lay a bean bag weight across your stomach before lifting your hips off the floor. (See the directions for making bean bag weights on pages 134–135.)

Thigh Highs

This exercise targets the muscles on the outside of the thighs and hips.
Keeping these muscles strong allows more efficient side-to-side movements, such as
those involved in dribbling a basketball, dancing, or kicking to the side in aikido.

What You Do

1. Lie on your side.

2. Straighten your bottom arm and place it under your head at your ear.

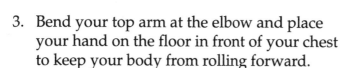

3. Bend your top arm at the elbow and place your hand on the floor in front of your chest to keep your body from rolling forward.

4. Lift your top leg straight up as far as it will go, making sure your toes and knee face front. Lower your leg to the starting position.

5. Repeat 8-12 times or until you get tired.

6. Switch sides and repeat.

Thigh Highs

(continued)

Variation—Thigh-High Challenge

This version of Thigh Highs is a lot harder to do because it involves lifting
your entire body, which requires many more muscles than just lifting your legs.
Balance and strength are both required for this activity.

What You Do

1. Lie on your right side with your legs straight on top of one another.
2. Bend your right arm and place your right elbow under your right shoulder.
3. Place your left hand on the floor in front of your stomach to keep your body from rolling forward.
4. Press down on your right elbow as you lift your hips off the floor, creating a straight line, as shown.
5. Lift your top leg as high as it will go, then lower it. Make sure you keep your toes and knee facing forward.
6. Repeat 10 times or until you feel tired, then switch sides.
7. For an added challenge, do this activity with bean bag weights strapped on your ankles. (See the directions for making bean bag weights on pages 134–135.)

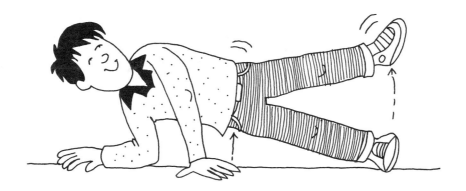

Floor Flying

This exercise requires the use of almost all the muscles located on the back side of your body.

What You Do

1. Lie on your stomach face down with your arms down at your sides.

2. Without moving your arms, gently lift your head and chest off the floor, as shown.

3. Return to your starting position and repeat 10 times.

These variations will add challenge to your Floor Flying workout.

Variation 1

1. Lie on your stomach face down with your arms extended above your head.

2. In a slow and controlled movement, lift one arm or one leg at a time as you lift your chest and head off the floor.

3. Keep your hips on the floor and your neck muscles relaxed.

4. Hold for a few seconds before returning to your starting position.

5. Repeat 8 times.

LIFT ONLY 1 ARM OR LEG AT A TIME

Floor Flying

(continued)

Variation 2

1. Lie on your stomach.

2. Relax the muscles in your legs and buttocks.

3. Slowly lift your upper body off the floor with your arms straight out at your sides like an airplane.

4. This is an advanced back exercise because you are lifting the upper body without support. Don't forget to breathe as you do this activity.

5. Return to your starting position. Repeat 10 times.

Variation 3

1. Lie on your stomach face down with your arms down at your sides.

2. Without moving your arms, gently lift your head and chest off the floor.

3. Keeping your legs straight and slightly apart, make a slight kicking motion as though you were swimming under water. (Do not kick vigorously!) Continue this slight and controlled kicking for 10 seconds.

Couch Kicks

This activity strengthens the front of your thighs. The quadriceps
are necessary for walking, running, leaping, jumping, kicking, swimming, and diving.

What You Do

1. Sit on the edge of a couch or chair. Slowly
   extend your right leg straight from your
   knee as though you were kicking a ball in
   slow motion. Slowly bring your right leg
   back to the starting position. Now perform
   this movement with your left leg. Alternate
   legs as you do Couch Kicks 10 times with
   each leg.

2. Now do Couch Kicks with both legs at the
   same time. Sit up straight and tall as you do
   them.

3. Try this exercise with bean bag weights
   around your ankles. (See the directions
   for making bean bag weights on pages
   134–135.)

4. Do as many Couch Kicks as you can, then
   try to do 4 more.

5. For an added challenge, reach for your toes
   with your opposite hand as you extend
   your legs.

80

Sock Hop

Sock Hop can be done quickly or slowly. Either way, your heart will beat faster.
Increasing your heart rate for extended periods of time on a regular basis
will help improve your cardiovascular fitness. You should be able
to talk without huffing and puffing as you do this exercise.

What You Do

1. Take your shoes off and wiggle your toes.

2. Stand on a carpeted surface.

3. Turn on the radio or play your favorite music on a cassette or CD.

4. Hop to the music in the following pattern:
   - Hop on your right foot 8 counts.
   - Hop on your left foot 8 counts.
   - Hop on your right foot 4 counts.
   - Hop on your left foot 4 counts.
   - Hop on your right foot 2 counts.
   - Hop on your left foot 2 counts.
   - Hop on your right foot 1 count.
   - Hop on your left foot 1 count.
   - Hop on your right foot 1 count.
   - Hop on your left foot 1 count.

5. Repeat the sequence until you begin to feel tired.

Keep the Beat

Try doing this fun exercise during commercials. Turn down the volume on your television and play your favorite marching music on a CD or cassette.

What You Do

1. Sit tall on the edge of a couch or chair.

2. March in place 8 times with your feet close together and your arms swinging at your sides.

3. Move your feet about 18 inches apart and keep marching in place for 8 more beats.

4. Place both hands on your knees. Stand up and sit down 2 times.

5. March in place 4 times with your feet close together.

6. March in place 4 times with your feet farther apart.

7. Stand up and sit down 2 times.

8. Repeat Keep the Beat until the commercial break is over.

Jig Jog

Here's another great exercise to increase your heart rate
and improve your cardiovascular fitness.

What You Do

1. Stand with your feet shoulder-width apart.

2. Move your hips side to side for 4 counts.

3. Jog in place or around the room for 4
    counts.

4. Alternate these two movements until you
    feel your heart beating faster.

5. For an added challenge, put your hands on
    your hips for the first 4 counts then raise
    your arms overhead on each jog.

6. You can really get creative with this
    exercise. Make up your own wacky move-
    ments to Jig Jog. Don't forget to cool down.
    You can do this by slowly walking around
    the room for a few minutes after you finish
    this exercise.

Posture Pleasers

The first version of this exercise strengthens your chest muscles and the second version works the muscles between your shoulder blades. Both sets of muscles contribute to better posture and a stronger upper body. Many sports and activities emphasize leg strength; these exercises will keep your upper body as strong as your lower body.

Variation 1—Chest Muscles
What You Do

1. Lie on your back with your knees bent and your feet flat on the floor close to your buttocks.

2. Your arms should be straight out to your sides, palms up.

3. Keeping your head on the floor, slowly lift your arms straight up, bringing your hands together above your chest.

4. Slowly lower your arms to your starting position.

5. Repeat 8 to 12 times or until you begin to feel tired.

6. For an added challenge, hold cans of beans, bean bag weights, or books in your hands while you do this exercise.

Posture Pleasers

(continued)

Variation 2—Shoulder Blades
What You Do

1. Drape yourself over a footstool and rest your chest on top of it. Bend your knees as shown. Keep your head, neck, and back in a straight line.

2. Let your arms hang down at your sides, hands pointing toward the floor, palms turned in toward the footstool.

3. Squeeze your shoulder blades together and slowly lift your arms straight up until they are level with your body. (Do not raise your arms any higher.)

4. Slowly lower your arms to the starting position.

5. Repeat 8 to 10 times or until you begin to feel tired.

6. For an added challenge, hold cans of beans, bean bags weights, or books in your hands as you do this exercise.

Easy Rider

This is a fun activity to do for short periods of time to get your blood circulating. It also requires good balance. Since your legs will be above your head, you should only perform this activity for a minute or two.

What You Do

1. Lie on the floor on your back. Put a pillow or rolled-up towel under your hips.

2. Bend your knees into your chest.

3. Your arms should be straight out at your sides with your palms facing down.

4. Circle your legs in a bicycle motion by bringing one leg up and bending it back over your chest, as you straighten the other leg.

5. Continue doing Easy Rider for one or two minutes.

6. For an added challenge, lift your hips off the floor and support them with your arms. Be sure to keep your weight on your shoulders, as shown, and NOT your neck!

Out and About

Jump and Jive

This is a fun way to increase your heart rate and improve your cardiovascular fitness while practicing coordination skills.

What You Do

1. In your yard, spread a garden hose into a straight line 10-15 feet in length.

2. Stand at one end of the hose. Straddle the hose with your feet shoulder-distance apart.

3. Jump up off the ground landing with your feet criss-crossed right over left over the hose on the count of 1. Jump back to the beginning position on count 2. Jump into a criss-crossed position with your left foot in front of your right foot on the count of 3. On count 4, jump back into your beginning position, straddling the hose with feet apart.

Jump and Jive

(continued)

4. Walk forward for 10 steps, stepping so that your right foot crosses the hose to the left side and your left foot crosses the hose to the right side. Each step is counted as 1.

5. Now repeat the jumps from step 3.

6. To finish, do 4 criss-cross jumps in place followed by 4 criss-cross steps until you reach the end of the hose. Turn around and repeat the sequence.

7. For an added challenge, speed up your stepping and jumping.

Body Roll

This is a relaxing exercise you can do whenever you are out and about.
Try it on a park bench or in the stadium at the ballpark.

What You Do

1. Sit on the edge of your seat with your arms hanging at your sides and your feet flat on the ground in front of you. Slowly drop your head forward and roll your spine down one inch at a time, bringing your torso into your chest, as shown.

2. Circle your wrists 3 times clockwise and 3 times counterclockwise as your arms hang by your sides.

3. Now unroll your torso and straighten your spine one inch at a time until you are sitting tall again.

4. Repeat until you feel relaxed.

5. For an added challenge, place your right ankle on your left knee, as shown, and then begin your body roll. Switch legs and repeat.

Side Saddle Stretch

This is a good stretch for the front of your thighs and your hips. When you sit for a long time, the muscles that flex your hips can also tighten your lower back. Stretching these muscles will help prevent lower-back pain.

What You Do

1. Sit on the edge of your seat with your feet flat on the floor in front of you.

2. While seated, pivot on your buttocks, making a quarter turn to your left.

3. Drop your right knee so it is pointing to the floor directly under your right hip, as shown. Your left leg should be bent with your left foot on the floor to help you keep your balance.

4. From this position, tuck your buttocks under, rolling your hip back until you feel a nice stretch in the thigh muscle of the right leg.

5. Hold this position for a count of 30 and then switch sides and repeat.

Torso Twisters

This simple stretch will help to relax the muscles in your back
and sides while traveling in a car or on an airplane.

What You Do

1. Sit tall in your seat with your feet flat on the floor.

2. Twist to the right, stretching your left arm across the front of your body. Try to stretch both arms until your hands grab your seat back (or the armrest on your right).

3. Return to your starting position and stretch both arms forward as far as you can.

4. Now twist to the left, stretching your right arm across the front of your body. Try to stretch both arms until your hands grab your seat back (or the armrest on your left).

5. Return to your starting position and stretch both arms forward as far as you can.

 # Chair Dance

This exercise increases your circulation and improves your coordination. After you have practiced it for a few minutes, try doing Chair Dance to the beat of your favorite music.

What You Do

1. Stand, feet together, facing the back of a chair. Place both hands on the back of the chair for balance.

2. Facing forward, step with your right foot so that it lands two to three feet out and to the right side.

3. Return to your starting position. Repeat the movement with your left foot.

4. For an added challenge, make a quarter turn away from the chair as you step away.

 # Ankle Antics

This exercise is a fun way to pass the time when you're sitting for a long period of time.

What You Do

1. Seated with your feet flat on the floor, lift both heels and return them to the floor 8 times.

2. Leaving your heels on the floor, lift your toes off the floor 8 times. Tap them to the floor on each count.

3. Repeat the heel lifts for 4 counts and follow with the toe lifts for 4 counts.

4. Alternate both movements for 2 counts.

5. Repeat the sequence 10-12 times.

Shoulder Shrugs

This is a relaxing exercise for your shoulders, neck, and upper back.
Before you do this activity, massage the muscles in these areas by
pressing down firmly with your fingers and rubbing in a circular motion.
This increases the circulation to these areas and allows the muscles to relax.

What You Do

1. Sit tall on the edge of your seat with your feet flat on the floor in front of you.

2. Slowly lift both shoulders up toward your ears as far as you can.

3. Without dropping your shoulders, squeeze your shoulder blades together as tightly as you can, as shown.

4. Now lower your shoulders and press them down and back as far as you can, as shown.

5. Round your shoulders forward and separate your shoulder blades, as shown.

6. Repeat the entire sequence 3 times. Reverse directions and repeat the sequence 4 times. Be sure to sit straight and maintain good posture.

DOWN
AND
BACK

95

Travel Tune-Up

Traveling in a car, bus, or airplane often involves sitting for long periods of time.
Not being able to move around can make your joints and muscles feel stiff.
This exercise allows you to adjust your position often, which helps
you feel better when you have to sit in a tight space.

What You Do

1. Wiggle your toes for a count of 10.

2. Circle your ankles 10 times clockwise and 10 times counterclockwise. Try circling one ankle clockwise and the other ankle counterclockwise at the same time.

3. Straighten and bend your knees as far forward as you can.

4. Tuck your buttocks under you, creating a "C" shape with your back, as shown. (Rest your arms on the sides of the chair seat or on the armrests.) Now push your buttocks out behind you, gently arching your back in the opposite direction.

5. Bend your elbows and press them behind you, squeezing your shoulder blades together. Then cross your arms around your chest and give yourself a big hug.

6. Lift and drop your shoulders one at a time.

7. Relax your shoulders while letting your head drop to one side. Try to lower your ear to the same shoulder. Very slowly reverse sides.

8. Drop your head forward. Put your hands behind your head and press forward gently until you feel a relaxing stretch at the back of your neck.

9. Repeat the sequence, working backwards from step 8 to step 1.

Nutrition and Recipes

Nutrition in a Nutshell

Eating a nutritious diet is a lot like putting together a winning sports team. The players on your healthy food team are called *nutrients*. They include carbohydrates, proteins, fats, vitamins, minerals, and water. Like the players on a team, each nutrient has specific functions but is required to interact with the others to carry out those functions.

Carbohydrates are the body's principal source of energy. There are two types of carbohydrates: simple and complex. Simple or "sugary" carbohydrates are found in foods like cookies, candy, and soda and contain little if any vitamins and minerals. Complex carbohydrates are found in foods such as cereal, bread, and pasta. These foods contain many important vitamins and minerals. The most nutritious varieties of cereal, bread, and pasta are made with whole wheat flour rather than white flour. When you are picking your players, complex carbohydrates are your best choice.

Proteins are used by the body to make tissues, cells, hair, bones, and all sorts of chemicals necessary for life. The best sources of protein come from foods in the meat and dairy groups, particularly egg whites and milk. Grains, fruits, and vegetables also contain proteins, but these are not as complete as the proteins found in meats and dairy foods.

Fats are a concentrated food source of energy. Many people consider fat to be a "bad food," but it is important to remember that some dietary fat is necessary to stay healthy. Fat helps maintain healthy skin and hair. Foods high in fat are unhealthy when you eat too much of them. When choosing fats for your healthy food team, choose foods that get their fat from plants (for example, vegetable oils and nuts) rather than animals.

Nutrition in a Nutshell

(continued)

Vitamins and minerals are contained in most foods. Vitamins are organic food substances that the body needs only in very small quantities but are essential for other nutrients to be effective. Minerals—such as calcium, iodine, and iron—are an essential part of all cells and body fluids. If you eat the recommended servings from each food group everyday, your diet should contain all the vitamins and minerals you need.

 Water makes up 50 to 70% of the human body and is, therefore, the most abundant compound in the body. Because the body does not store water, water must be replaced continually. It is important to drink a sufficient amount of water each day. The body also obtains water from foods and other beverages you consume. Water is used by the body to regulate temperature, to transport nutrients, and as a body lubricant.

Calories and Healthful Eating

The term "calorie" is used to describe both the energy output of humans and the fuel or energy value of food. Physical activity "burns off" or uses up calories, and the food we eat contains calories. The caloric value of food differs depending on its type: 1 gram of pure protein contains 4 calories, 1 gram of pure fat contains 9 calories, and 1 gram of pure carbohydrate contains 4 calories.

When you eat more food than is recommended for your age, size, and activity level, the calories from the extra food are stored in your body as fat. When you don't eat enough food each day for your age, size, and activity level, you will lose weight, feel tired, and may even become ill. Don't worry if you eat too much or too little once in awhile. The idea is to try to follow the guidelines for healthy eating "most of the time."

Kids should not go on diets. If you feel like you weigh too much for your age and size, check with a health professional to make sure. If weight loss truly is needed, he or she can guide you in the right direction. Sensible weight loss involves increasing your activity level and cutting back on foods high in fat and sugar.

What Is The Food Guide Pyramid?

The Food Guide Pyramid was approved in 1992 by the United States Department of Agriculture as the basic guide for maintaining a healthy diet. The pyramid suggests the number of daily servings needed in each of six major food groups. Daily servings required in the food pyramid vary according to individual needs at different stages of growth and activity levels.

The recipes in *Movin' and Groovin'* have been selected according to the recommendations given in the Food Guide Pyramid. Thus, foods containing fats, oils, and refined sugars have been used sparingly, while foods from the bread, cereal, rice, and pasta group have been emphasized. Recipe ingredients that contain sugar and fat can be substituted with sugar-free, fat-free, and low-fat products, if you prefer.

The Food Guide Pyramid

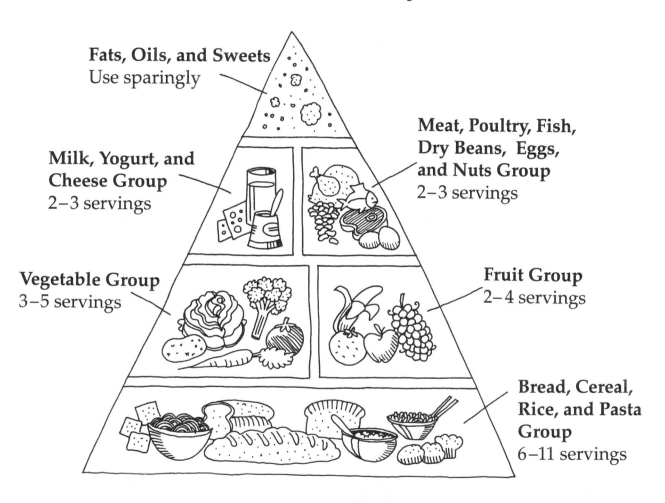

Fats, Oils, and Sweets
Use sparingly

Meat, Poultry, Fish, Dry Beans, Eggs, and Nuts Group
2–3 servings

Milk, Yogurt, and Cheese Group
2–3 servings

Vegetable Group
3–5 servings

Fruit Group
2–4 servings

Bread, Cereal, Rice, and Pasta Group
6–11 servings

The Food Guide Pyramid:
A Guide to Daily Food Choices

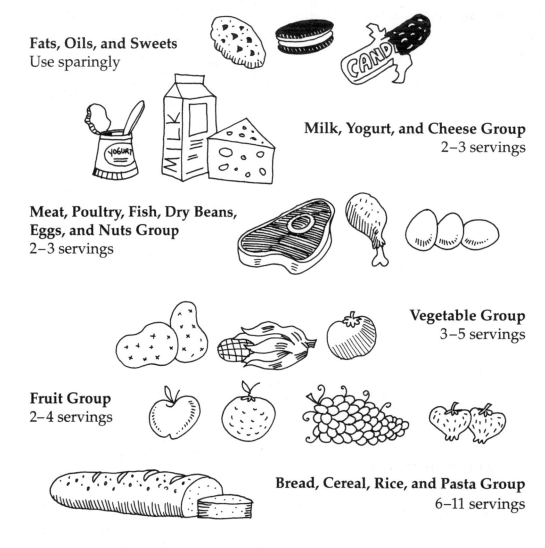

Fats, Oils, and Sweets
Use sparingly

Milk, Yogurt, and Cheese Group
2–3 servings

Meat, Poultry, Fish, Dry Beans, Eggs, and Nuts Group
2–3 servings

Vegetable Group
3–5 servings

Fruit Group
2–4 servings

Bread, Cereal, Rice, and Pasta Group
6–11 servings

Source: U.S. Department of Agriculture/U.S. Department of Health and Human Services

How Much Is One Serving?

One serving of the bread, cereal, rice, and pasta group is:

- 1 slice of bread,
- 1 ounce of ready-to-eat cereal,
- 1/2 cup of cooked cereal, rice, or pasta, or
- 3–4 small crackers

  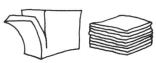

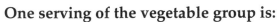

One serving of the milk, yogurt, and cheese group is:

- 1 cup of milk or yogurt,
- $1^1/2$ ounces of natural cheese, or
- 2 ounces of processed cheese

One serving of the vegetable group is:

- 1 cup of raw, leafy vegetables,
- 1/2 cup of other vegetables, cooked or raw, or
- 3/4 cup of vegetable juice

One serving of the meat, poultry, fish, dry beans, eggs, and nuts group is:

- 2–3 ounces of cooked lean meat, poultry, or fish,
- 1/2 cup of cooked dry beans,
- 1 egg, or
- 2 tablespoons of peanut butter

One serving of the fruit group is:

- 1 medium apple, banana, or orange,
- 1/2 cup of cooked or canned unsweetened fruit, or
- 3/4 cup of fruit juice

The Snack Scoreboard

Here's a fun game to play that will help you make healthier food choices.
The next time you have a snack attack, check the Snack Scoreboard first.

Here's How to Play

1. Most packaged foods have nutritional labels. Locate the label on your favorite snack food.

2. Take a pencil and paper and score the food with the following point system:
   - 1 point for each percent of fat
   - 1 point for each 100 milligrams of sodium
   - 1 point for each gram of simple sugar
   - 5 points if it contains coconut or palm oils
   - 5 points if there is more package material than food
   - 5 points if it contains more than 3 milligrams of caffeine
   - 5 points if it contains artificial colors

3. Scoreboard ranges:
   - 1–25 points: Snack Jackpot!
   - 26–40 points: Not so bad, not so good.
   - 41–50 points: Borderline
   - 51+ points: Snack hazard—eat or drink sparingly

The Snack Scoreboard
(continued)

Examples:

Pretzels		Cola
0	% Fat score	0
5	Sodium score	.5
0	Sugar score	39
0	coconut palm oils	0
0	Package score	5
0	Caffeine score	5
0	Artificial color score	5
5	Total points	54.5

Pretzels hit the Snack Jackpot! Cola could be hazardous to your health; drink sparingly!

Nutrition Tips

The Food Guide Pyramid is a basic guideline for healthful eating. If your daily meals don't correspond exactly to the numbers on the Pyramid, don't worry. The numbers give you goals to strive for.

Here are some helpful hints for healthy eating habits:

1. Eat a variety of foods when you are hungry.

2. Stop eating when you are full.

3. Try new foods.

4. Try to eat fruits and vegetables of many colors, such as carrots, strawberries, corn, kiwi fruit, and potatoes.

5. Help your mom or dad with the grocery shopping and meal preparation.

6. Don't skip breakfast.

7. Snack often with foods that score well on the "Snack Scoreboard."

8. Avoid skipping meals.

9. Make air-popped popcorn for TV time.

10. Pack healthful snacks ahead of time when you fly on an airplane or take long trips in the car. Choose:
    - foods in their most natural forms (for example, whole wheat bread offers more nutrition than white bread).
    - fresh fruits and vegetables, since they contain more nutrients than those which are canned or processed.
    - low-fat or nonfat milk, cheese, and yogurt.
    - meats and poultry with less fat and skin.
    - snack foods with less fat, sugar, salt, additives, and caffeine.

Label Logic

Whenever you make food choices, use "label logic."
Here are some questions you can ask yourself when selecting food products:

- What are the first three things the manufacturer wants you to know about their product?

- Are any claims deliberately misleading? If so, why?

- What is the serving size?

- How many servings are there? Is it easy to figure out? If not, why?

- How many calories are there in one serving?

- Where do the calories come from? Do they total the calories per serving?

		Example: frosted corn cereal	
Carbohydrate	# of grams X 4 =	Carbohydrate	45 grams X 4 = 180
Protein	# of grams X 4 =	Protein	5 grams X 4 = 20
Fat	# of grams X 9 =	Fat	3 grams X 9 = 27
Total number of calories		Total number of calories = 227	

- What percentage of the calories comes from fat? How does this compare to the "% Daily Value"?

- How many grams of carbohydrate are simple sugars?

- Does this food provide good nutritional value? If not, is it worth the FUN of eating it?

Banana Muffin Munchies

Whip up a batch of these muffins and eat them while they're still warm.

What You Need

- 1 tablespoon margarine
- 1 cup sugar
- 1 ripe, mashed banana
- 2 egg whites
- 1 cup flour

- 1/2 cup whole wheat flour
- 1 teaspoon baking soda
- 1/2 teaspoon salt
- 1/3 cup nonfat milk

What You Do

1. Preheat the oven to 350°.

2. Cream the margarine and sugar together until the mixture is smooth.

3. Stir in the banana and the egg whites.

4. In a separate bowl, mix both flours, baking soda, and salt.

5. Add the margarine mixture to the dry ingredients, adding a little milk at a time. Don't overmix.

6. Pour mix in a muffin tin lined with paper cups.

7. Bake for 20-30 minutes or until the tops are golden brown.

Bran Muffin Mania

These muffins are not only delicious, they're also good for you!

What You Need

- 1 cup whole bran cereal
- 1 cup all-purpose flour
- 2 tablespoons wheat germ
- 2 tablespoons toasted sunflower seeds
- 1 teaspoon baking soda
- 1 beaten egg
- 3/4 cup buttermilk
- 1/4 cup brown sugar
- 1/4 cup cooking oil
- 2 tablespoons honey

What You Do

1. In a large bowl, mix the bran cereal, flour, wheat germ, sunflower seeds, and baking soda.

2. In a separate bowl, combine the egg, buttermilk, brown sugar, oil, and honey.

3. Add the liquid ingredients to the dry ingredients in the larger bowl.

4. Gently stir (do not beat) until all the ingredients are moistened.

5. Fill a greased or paper-lined muffin pan 2/3 full with the batter.

6. Bake in a preheated 400° oven for 15-20 minutes.

Cinnamon French Toast

Try this yummy recipe and serve it with syrup or jam.

What You Need

- 2 beaten eggs
- 1/2 cup skimmed milk
- 2 tablespoons margarine
- 1/4 teaspoon vanilla
- 1/8 teaspoon ground cinnamon
- 6 slices of bread

What You Do

1. Beat the eggs, milk, vanilla, and cinnamon together in a bowl.

2. Dip a piece of bread into the mixture. Be sure both sides are well coated.

3. Melt the margarine in a large skillet. Cook three slices of the bread on one side for 2-3 minutes or until they turn golden brown.

4. Use a spatula to turn the bread to the other side. Cook until golden brown.

5. Repeat for the other three slices of bread.

Fresh Fruit Fiesta

Top this treat with your favorite fruit-flavored yogurt.

What You Need

- 2 medium oranges
- 1 sliced banana
- 1 cup cubed honeydew melon
- 1 cup cubed cantaloupe
- 1/2 cup seedless green grapes
- 1 cup halved strawberries

- 1 cup blueberries or raspberries
- 1/3 cup honey
- 1/2 teaspoon shredded lemon peel
- 1 tablespoon lemon juice
- 1/8 teaspoon ground nutmeg

What You Do

1. In a large bowl, peel and cut the orange into sections. Pour the juice into a separate bowl.

2. Add the rest of the fruit except for the berries.

3. Add the honey, lemon peel, lemon juice and nutmeg to the orange juice.

4. Pour the juice mixture over the fruit. Chill for 3-4 hours.

5. Before serving, gently stir in the berries.

Granola Crunch

Make this up ahead of time for those times when the hungries hit!

What You Need

- 5 cups oats
- 1 cup wheat germ
- 1 cup honey
- 1 cup sliced almonds
- 1 cup raisins
- 1/2 cup vegetable oil

What You Do

1. Mix the dry ingredients together in a large bowl.

2. In a saucepan, combine the honey and oil. Heat this mixture over a low heat until warm.

3. Mix the honey and oil with the dry ingredients.

4. Spread the mixture on two large baking sheets.

5. Bake in a preheated 275° oven for one hour or until brown. Stir occasionally.

Simple Scrambled Eggs

Here's a simple recipe for a breakfast you can make for yourself and your family.

What You Need

- 6 eggs
- 1/3 cup skim milk
- 1 tablespoon margarine
- 1/4 teaspoon salt
- dash pepper

What You Do

1. In a small bowl, beat together the eggs, milk, salt, and pepper.

2. In a large skillet, melt the margarine and pour in the egg mixture.

3. Do not stir the egg mixture until it begins to set or firm on the bottom and around the edges.

4. Use a large spatula or spoon to lift and fold the partially cooked eggs so that the uncooked part flows underneath.

5. Cook over medium heat for 2-3 minutes.

6. Avoid overcooking the eggs—they should be slightly moist and glossy.

Serves 4

Apple-Raisin Riot

Mix up a batch of this sensational salad to go with your favorite sandwich.

What You Need

- 2 golden delicious apples
- 1/3 cup chopped walnuts
- 1/2 cup raisins
- 1 cup sliced celery
- 2 tablespoons lemon juice
- 3/4 cup low-fat mayonnaise

What You Do

1. Cut the apples in cubes and place them in a bowl. (Don't forget to remove the stems and cores.)

2. Add the next four ingredients to the apples.

3. Add the mayonnaise and mix gently.

4. Chill until you are ready to eat your Apple-Raisin Riot.

Try This

Add 2 cups of cubed chicken or turkey to turn this salad into a main dish meal.

Chicken 1-2-3

This recipe is exactly that—easy as 1-2-3!

What You Need

- 1 chicken, cut up (skin removed)
- 1 bottle of low-fat Russian salad dressing
- 1 jar (18 ounces) apricot preserves
- 1 package dry onion soup mix
- 1 teaspoon margarine

What You Do

1. Grease the bottom of a 9 x 13-inch baking dish with the margarine.

2. Place the chicken in a baking dish. Combine the salad dressing, apricot preserves, and onion soup. Mix well and pour over the chicken.

3. Bake uncovered at 350° for one hour. Baste frequently.

Chili and Corn Casserole

As this casserole cooks, the muffin mixture will puff up, making a golden crust.

What You Need

- 2 cans (15 ounces) chili with beans
- 1 can (12 ounces) Mexican-style corn
- 1 package corn muffin mix
- 1 egg
- 1/3 cup skim milk

What You Do

1. Drain the corn and combine it with the chili in a saucepan. Heat slowly.

2. Pour the mixture into a greased 9 x 13-inch baking dish.

3. In a separate bowl, combine the muffin mix, egg, and milk. Stir until mixed.

4. Spread the muffin mixture evenly over the chili.

5. Bake in a preheated 450° oven for 20 minutes until the crust is golden brown.

Hula Hula Chicken

A hint of pineapple gives this chicken an incredible flavor.

What You Need

- 1 chicken, cut up
- 3/4 cup unsweetened pineapple juice
- 1/4 cup low-sodium soy sauce
- 1/4 teaspoon ground ginger
- 1/4 teaspoon black pepper

What You Do

1. Place the chicken in a 9 x 13-inch baking dish, skin-side down.

2. Combine the other ingredients, mix well, and pour over the chicken.

3. Bake in a preheated 350° oven for 55-60 minutes. Baste often.

Marvelous Macaroni and Cheese

An easy-to-make dinner for macaroni and cheese fans.

What You Need

- 8-ounce package of elbow macaroni
- 1 teaspoon mustard
- 1 cup skim milk
- 1 cup shredded low-fat American cheese
- salt and pepper to taste
- paprika

What You Do

1. Cook the macaroni according to the directions on the package. Drain the cooked macaroni.

2. Mix the mustard into the milk. Combine with the cooked macaroni.

3. Stir in the cheese. (Save some of the cheese to sprinkle on the top.)

4. Pour the mixture into a greased 9 x 13-inch baking dish.

5. Top with the remaining cheese and a sprinkle of paprika

6. Bake uncovered in a 350° oven for 30-35 minutes.

Muffin Burgers

These burgers are perfect for lunch, dinner, or an after-school snack.

What You Need

- 1 pound lean ground beef
- 1 package taco seasoning mix ($1^1/_4$ ounces)
- 1/2 cup water
- 4 English muffins
- 1 cup grated low-fat cheddar cheese

What You Do

1. Brown the ground beef and drain the fat.

2. Add the taco mix and water. Simmer until all of the liquid is absorbed (about 12-15 minutes).

3. Split the English muffins and place them face up on a cookie sheet.

4. Put a large spoonful of meat on top of each muffin half.

5. Sprinkle the cheese on top of the meat.

6. Bake in a preheated 350° oven for 10-15 minutes until the cheese melts.

Pasta Twists

Even if you don't like broccoli, you'll love this pasta dish!

What You Need

- 1 onion, diced
- 2 teaspoons margarine
- 1 clove garlic, minced
- 1 16-ounce can whole tomatoes
- 1/4 teaspoon dried basil
- 1 tablespoon parsley
- 1 10-ounce package frozen chopped broccoli, thawed
- 1 8-ounce package pasta twists
- 2 tablespoons grated Parmesan cheese

What You Do

1. Saute the onion and garlic in the margarine for 5 minutes over a low heat.

2. Add the tomatoes, basil, and parsley. Cover and cook for 5 minutes.

3. Add the broccoli, cover and cook for 10 minutes.

4. Cook the pasta twists according to the package directions. Drained the cooked pasta.

5. Toss the pasta with the sauce. Top with the cheese.

Peppy Pizza

Here's a delicious treat to make after school or for dinner.

What You Need

- 1 cup low-fat mozzarella cheese
- 1/4 cup low-fat jack cheese
- $1^1/_2$ cups tomato sauce
- 1 small green bell pepper
- 12-inch pizza dough round (fresh or frozen)

What You Do

1. Preheat the oven to 450°.

2. Shred the mozzarella and jack cheeses.

3. Cut the top off the bell pepper. Scoop out the seeds, and rinse the inside of the bell pepper in cold water. Slice the bell pepper into thin strips.

4. Place the pizza on a flat pizza pan. Cover the pizza with the tomato sauce.

5. Sprinkle the cheeses on top of the tomato sauce.

6. Add the green pepper strips.

7. Place the pizza in the middle of the oven. Bake for 12-15 minutes or until the cheese starts to bubble.

Tortilla Treats

For an easy, south-of-the-border treat, try this tasty recipe.

What You Need

- 1 6-inch flour tortilla
- 2 tablespoons grated low-fat jack cheese
- 1 tablespoon salsa

What You Do

1. Lay the tortilla flat on a kitchen counter.

2. Place the grated cheese in the center of the tortilla.

3. Add the salsa.

4. Fold in both sides and roll it up, as shown.

5. Place the stuffed tortilla on a paper plate. Cover with wax paper.

6. Microwave on high for one minute.

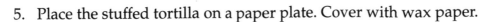
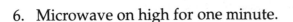

South-of-the-Border Turkey Tacos

You can substitute ground beef for the turkey if you prefer.

What You Need

- 1 pound ground turkey
- 1 tablespoon oil
- 1 package taco seasoning mix (1¹/₄ ounces)
- shredded lettuce
- grated low-fat cheddar cheese
- chopped tomato
- taco shells

What You Do

1. In a skillet, brown the ground turkey in oil. Drain any oil left in the skillet.

2. Add the seasoning mix and amount of water called for on the package to the turkey mixture.

3. Bring to a boil. Reduce the heat and simmer uncovered for 15-20 minutes.

4. Stir occasionally until all the liquid is absorbed.

5. Spoon several tablespoons of the turkey mixture in a taco shell. Top with the remaining ingredients.

Tuna Noodle Bake

The crispy chow mein noodles give this casserole an added crunch.

What You Need

- 1/4 cup margarine
- 1/4 cup flour
- 2 cups skim milk
- 1 cup shredded low-fat American cheese
- 1 can (3 ounces) crispy chow mein noodles
- 1 package (8 ounces) thin pasta noodles
- 1 can (7 ounces) tuna, drained
- 1 cup green peas

What You Do

1. Cook the pasta according to package directions. Drain the pasta and set it aside.

2. Melt the margarine in a saucepan over low heat.

3. Stir in the flour and mix until blended.

4. Slowly stir in the milk. Cook, stirring often, until the sauce is thick.

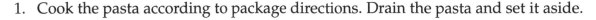

5. Add the cheese to the sauce.

6. Combine the tuna, cooked pasta, peas, crispy noodles, and sauce. Pour into a greased 9 x 13-inch casserole dish. Bake in a preheated 350° oven for 30 minutes.

Halibut and Vegetable Duo

This tasty recipe combines carrots, celery, and onions to create a delicious topping.

What You Need

- 2 pounds halibut fillets
- 1 teaspoon salt
- 1/4 teaspoon paprika
- 1/4 teaspoon pepper
- 3 carrots
- 3 stalks celery
- 5 green onions
- 1 tablespoon lemon juice

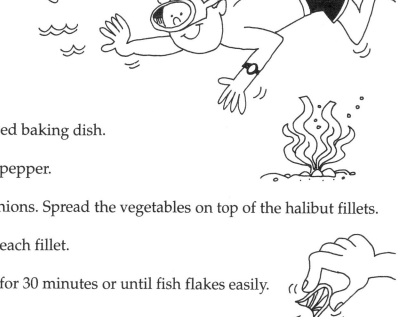

What You Do

1. Place the halibut in an ungreased baking dish.

2. Season with salt, paprika, and pepper.

3. Chop the carrots, celery, and onions. Spread the vegetables on top of the halibut fillets.

4. Sprinkle lemon juice on top of each fillet.

5. Bake in a preheated 350° oven for 30 minutes or until fish flakes easily.

Chicken Fajitas

Here's a recipe that's easy to put together for a delicious lunch or dinner.

What You Need

- 6 chicken breast halves (skinned and boned)
- 3 tablespoons vegetable oil
- 1/8 teaspoon paprika
- 8-inch flour tortillas
- one jar of salsa

What You Do

1. Cut the chicken breasts into one-inch strips.

2. Saute the chicken strips in heated oil. Stir often. Cook until the chicken is tender and loses its pink color.

3. Sprinkle with paprika.

4. Place a spoonful of chicken on each tortilla and top with salsa.

5. Fold the tortilla around the filling and place seam-side down on a serving plate. Enjoy!

Tuna Ziti Salad

Try this delicious salad using cooked turkey or chicken instead of tuna if you prefer.

What You Need

- 1 package of ziti (8 ounces)
- 1 jar (7 ounces) roasted red peppers (drained)
- 1 small red onion
- 1/2 cup frozen peas (thawed and drained)
- 1/3 cup bottled, low-fat Italian salad dressing
- 1 can (13 ounces) solid white tuna (drained and broken into chunks)
- lettuce

What You Do

1. Cook the ziti according to the directions on the package. Pour the cooked ziti into a strainer. Cool the pasta by running cold water over it. Drain well.

2. Place the cooked ziti in a large bowl. Cut the peppers into thin strips and add to the pasta.

3. Add the onions, peas, and salad dressing. Mix well.

4. Gently fold the tuna into the pasta.

5. Chill for several hours and then serve on a bed of lettuce.

Apple Dips

This easy-to-make dip is a tasty addition to crisp, crunchy apple slices.

What You Need

- 8-ounce carton of plain yogurt
- 1/2 cup peach preserves
- 1/8 teaspoon ground cinnamon
- apple slices

What You Do

1. Stir together the yogurt, preserves, and cinnamon.

2. Chill the mixture for 24 hours.

3. When ready to serve, cut an apple in slices, discarding the core.

4. Dip each apple slice in the apple dip and enjoy!

128

Fruity Tootie Yogurt Treat

Try this refreshing drink on a hot summer day.

What You Need

- 1 cup nonfat plain yogurt
- 1/4 cup peach nectar
- 1/4 cup frozen orange juice concentrate
- 1/2 cup chopped fresh fruit, such as bananas or strawberries

What You Do

1. Put all the ingredients in a blender.

2. Blend on medium until smooth. Enjoy!

PEACH NECTAR

129

Muncha Buncha Popcorn

Here's a delicious, easy-to-make snack that's good anytime.

What You Need

- 1/4 cup margarine
- 1/2 teaspoon dried Italian seasoning
- 1/4 teaspoon garlic powder
- 8 cups warmed popped popcorn
- 1/3 cup grated Parmesan cheese

What You Do

1. Stir margarine in a saucepan until melted.

2. Add the Italian seasoning and garlic powder.

3. Toss with the popped popcorn to coat evenly.

4. Add the Parmesan cheese and toss to coat evenly.

Pumpkin Seed Snackaroos

Try making this delicious snack that's great to munch on any time and any place.

What You Need

- 4 cups fresh pumpkin seeds
- 2 tablespoons vegetable oil
- salt to taste

What You Do

1. Wipe the fibers from the pumpkin seeds, but don't wash them.

2. Pour the vegetable oil over the pumpkin seeds.

3. Toss the pumpkin seeds to coat them evenly.

4. Spread the seeds onto two large baking sheets. Sprinkle with salt.

5. Bake in a preheated 350° oven until the seeds turn golden brown (about 30 minutes).

Snack Attack Mix

Mix up a batch of this yummy treat to munch on while you're doing your homework or reading a good book.

What You Need

- 1 cup each of any of your favorite bite-size cereal such as:
  - corn cereal
  - oat cereal
  - rice cereal
  - wheat cereal
- 1/2 cup honey roasted peanuts
- 1 cup pretzel sticks
- garlic salt or garlic powder (optional)

What You Do

1. Mix all the ingredients together. Sprinkle with garlic salt or garlic powder, if desired.

2. Gobble it up.

Veggie Wedgies

Next time you're hungry, try this simple-to-make sandwich.

What You Need

- 1 piece pita bread
- low-fat cream cheese, softened
- cucumber, thinly sliced
- sliced, low-fat Swiss cheese
- alfalfa sprouts
- tomato, thinly sliced

What You Do

1. Cut the pita bread in half.

2. Spread a thin layer of cream cheese on the pita halves.

3. Add the cucumber, Swiss cheese, alfalfa sprouts, and tomato slices.

4. Cut the pita into wedges as shown.

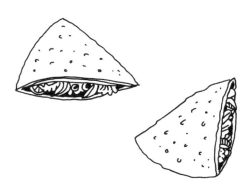

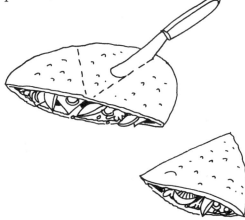

Make Your Own Bean Bag Weights

Materials Needed for Two Bean Bag Weights

- 4 cups of dried beans (two pounds)
- 4 pieces of $4^1/4$" x $12^1/2$" cotton fabric (pattern supplied on page 135)
- 6 double strips of hook-and-loop cloth fastening tape pieces of self-sticking fabric tape
  - 4 pieces 4" in length
  - 2 pieces $3^1/4$" in length
- sewing machine and thread

Instructions for One Bean Bag Weight

1. Position pattern on a folded piece of fabric and cut around it. (You can use fabric chalk to trace around the pattern, if you like.) Cut out four pieces of fabric $4^1/4$" x $12^1/2$".

2. Pin two pieces of material together on one $12^1/2$" side, right sides facing each other. Stitch the two pieces together, leaving a 1/2" seam allowance.

3. Open up material and press seam open. Turn fabric under 1/8" on one 8" side and press to create a finished edge when the material is right side up.

4. Position two of the 4" pieces of hook-and-loop tape on the pattern side of the fabric with the short ends meeting the unfinished edge on the 4" side (figure 4). The tapes should be parallel and leave room at the bottom for a 1/2" seam allowance. Pin the tape in place. Fold material along seam with pattern side in.

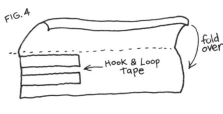

FIG. 4

Hook & Loop tape

fold over

5. Pin tape side and long side of the fabric together. Stitch these two sides, leaving the other 4" side open. Turn the material right side out.

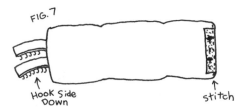

FIG. 7

Hook Side Down

stitch

6. Fill material with two cups of beans. Pin open end closed.

7. Pin one of the $3^1/4$" pieces of hook-and-loop tape along open end of material, making sure the hooks and loops face each other when weight is in place around ankle. Tape should be placed against open end (figure 7). Stitch, making sure seam catches both tape and turned-under edges of cloth.

Make Your Own Bean Bag Weights

(continued)

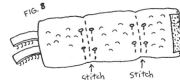

FIG. 8

stitch   stitch

8. Divide beans into three equal sections within the material. Pin and stitch to keep beans from shifting around (figure 8).

Repeat steps 2–8 to make a second bean bag weight. You should be able to strap the weights around your ankles, anchoring them securely with the hook-and-loop tape strips. Don't strap the weights on too tightly.

Note: If you don't have access to a sewing machine, you can fill a large tube sock with beans and attach rubber bands on both ends to keep the beans centered. Use the loose ends to tie the weight around your ankle.

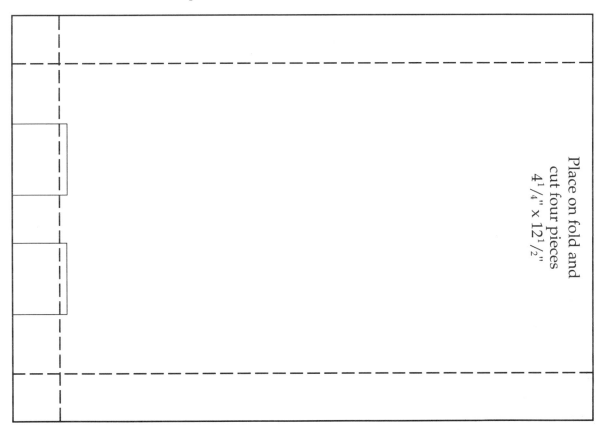

Place on fold and cut four pieces
$4^1/4$" x $12^1/2$"

About the Authors

Peggy Buchanan holds an M.A. in Physical Education from the University of California and is a Certified Fitness Professional. She taught high school physical education for seven years prior to becoming a Jazzercise® instructor and trainer in 1979. She has worked with fitness professional Covert Bailey and has coauthored *The Know More Diet*, a nutrition program for adults and children.

Linda Schwartz is the author of more than eighty books for children, including the award-winning titles *The Safety Book for Active Kids* and *What Do You Think?—A Kid's Guide to Dealing with Daily Dilemmas*. She holds an M.A. in Administration and Supervision from California State University Northridge and taught for ten years before founding The Learning Works in 1976.